FINDING MY FOOTPRINTS

David Cooke was born in 1953 in Wokingham, although his family comes from the West of Ireland. In 1977, while still an undergraduate at Nottingham University, he received a Gregory Award. His poems and reviews have been published widely in the UK, Ireland, and beyond. *Finding my Footprints* brings together a generous selection of those poems in which he explores his Irish Catholic inheritance.

By the Same Author

Brueghel's Dancers
In the Distance
Work Horses
A Slow Blues: Poems: 1972-2012
A Murmuration
After Hours
Reel to Reel
Slippage: Poems 2013-2018
Staring at a Hoopoe
Sicilian Elephants

FINDING MY FOOTPRINTS

David Cooke

The High Window

First published in the UK in 2022 by The High Window Press
3 Grovely Close
Peatmoor
Swindon
SN5 5DN
Email: abbeygatebooks@yahoo.co.uk

The right of David Cooke to be identified as the author of this work has been asserted by him in accordance with Copyright, Designs and Patent Act, 1988.
© David Cooke 2022
ISBN: 9798430140496

All rights reserved. No part of this book may be reproduced or transmitted in any form or by any means, electronic or mechanical, including photocopying, recording, or by any information storage and retrieval system, without permission in writing from the copyright owner. This book may not be lent, hired out, resold or otherwise disposed of by way of trade in any form of binding or cover other than that in which it is published, without prior consent of the publishers.

Designed and typeset in Palatino Linotype
by The High Window Press.
Printed and bound by Amazon KDP

do na glúine beo agus marbh

Contents

JOHNSFORTH

Fenians 13
In Search of Lost Time 14
Visiting 15
Down 16
Hill-fort 17
Cows 18
Holidays 19
A House in Mayo 20
Easter 1966 21
A Waldorf Salad 22
The Dresser 23
The Wren Boy 24
Goliath 25
The Morris Minor 26
The Gift 28
Respects 29
The Leaving Cert 30
Travellers 32
Johnsforth 34
Epilogue 36

MIGRANTS

Annus Mirabilis 39
In the Forbury Gardens 40
Songs He Sang Her 42
Coronation Street 43
Biscuits 44
Money 46
The House on Orchard Street 47
St James Primary, Reading 48
Grammar School 49
'Mens Sana in Corpore Sano' 50

Movement to Music *51*
A New Shirt *52*
Summer of '69 *53*
When Smokey Sings *54*
Stepping Out *55*
Gasometers *56*
Oscar Wilde Walk *57*
Peggy *58*
Migrants *59*
A Wet Break *60*

SHADOW BOXING

Work Horses *63*
Ascendants *64*
My Father the Pragmatist *65*
Your Chair *68*
Work *69*
Working Holidays *70*
The Night Out *72*
Gambler *73*
Shadow Boxing *74*
The Advice *75*
Navvies *76*
Thrift *77*
Hospital *78*
Memorial *79*
To My Father *80*
Family History *81*
Uprooted *82*
Caversham *83*
Caversham Revisited *84*
Apocryphal *85*

FAITH OF OUR FATHERS

Mischief *89*
Faith of Our Fathers *90*
The Master Builders *91*
Lives of the Saints *92*
Playtime *93*
Going to Mass *94*
The Latin Lesson *95*
Catechism *96*
Pater Noster *98*
Schooldays *99*
Out of Bounds *100*
Ships *102*
Luther *103*
In the Middle of the Way *104*
Fathers *106*
Calvin's Geneva *107*
On the Front *108*
On My Daughter's Conversion to Islam *109*
Beginnings *110*
Pilgrims *111*

AFTER HOURS

An Open Drawer *115*
Learning Irish *116*
Ó Direáin *117*
Occitan *118*
Local Music *119*
Empty Nests *120*
The Fly Past *122*
Last orders *123*
Redundancy *124*
Chemo *126*
Routines *127*
The Home *128*

Whiskey   *129*
31 Garnett Street   *130*
Effects   *131*
French Park   *132*
Going Home   *133*
The Tide   *134*
Valediction   *135*
Connacht   *136*

Afterword: How a Heart Breaks   *138*

JOHNSFORTH

i.m. Peter and Ellen McManus

FENIANS

It's the back end of a summer in the early
nineteen-sixties. We are waiting, the three of us,
in front of a gate that creaks between two worlds:
my sister so small I can hardly see her;
my brother Martin, who is also *Máirtín* –
though when I call him across the fields
I am mocked by cousins for the glottal stop
that makes them think I'm Cockney.

But mostly, we have all three gone native
and, like the Norman barons, the generations of Fitzes,
are now more Irish than the Irish themselves.
Adopting country circumlocutions,
we say *I do be* and *I'm after*.
We have learned the words of rebel songs.

It's the back end of a summer –
and behind us I see a whitewashed house,
its geraniums doing the best they can
in paint pot planters, the hens stepping warily,
as they look for places to hide their eggs.

Soon neighbours and uncles and aunts
will come to say goodbye to the *visitors*.
They will give us silver because we are children,
holding on to our hands. There are coins
with the heads of kings and a queen
and the ones we prefer with fishes, horses, bulls.
We can take them home
as souvenirs, but won't be able to spend them.

IN SEARCH OF LOST TIME

From the north of France to Mayo's a stretch,
but in the way that often one thing leads
to another I got there reading Proust –
or, if I'm honest, by struggling again
to read him beyond his hero's bedtime.

Buttoned up, fretful, a delicate child,
he had never dammed a stream with sods
or pulled up a ladder into the hay
where he had his lair and listened to rain
clattering down onto a hayshed roof.

Accumulating his endless pages
– an invalid and a scribbler, cooped up
in his cork-lined room – it wasn't the smell
of bread, baked in a pot in the embers,
that took Proust back to his earliest years

but a madeleine soaking in a cup
of weak tea. Free-falling into the past,
he never mentions creamery butter,
eggs with shells streaked in dirt, or the sizzle
and spit of sausages seasoned in smoke.

Lights out plunged him into creaks and shadows
and, on the nights he missed his mother's kiss,
an agony of sleeplessness. Voices
climbed the stairwell. In a three-room cottage
I awakened when the *craic* was mighty.

VISITING

When I first came on a visit
to your limewashed house
– a clean-kneed child from town –
your two great fists

impressed me, for they
were ponderous chunks
of granite, notched
carelessly for fingers

and which, at your own willed
creation, you had torn
from the heart of the land.
Yes, I knew then how

you had risen and, separate,
had kept on walking.
I was almost frightened
to be your friend, but still

am running so breathlessly
beside you, as you stride
onwards, the castle of yourself,
across rough fields

of thistle and clover.
And the dog is running
before us and laughter
creates a flawless sky.

DOWN

On long afternoons at Johnsforth
I lay down and listened. My ear
to the ground, I sensed far off
a thunder of horses trapped –
my animals burdened with death
and the weight of the hills.

For though I roamed quite freely
across that homely terrain,
my grandfather plagued me with tales
of *swally holes*, he called them,
a nothingness opening up
beneath my vagrant, careless steps.

I imagined the way it might feel
to sink through hurtling dark,
a child lost and endlessly falling
beyond all reach of rescuing hands,
my tiny cries absorbed
into the buzz of ancestral voices.

HILL-FORT

Evening, and small fields
are assigned to shadows,
the hills smudged dully
against residual sky.

The mournful call of a curlew,
distant, is finally
no more than the sky's soft
pulse. Night draws in

and the mind is a function
of its failing light;
it makes out smoke
from a further camp,

the sense of it borne
upon a stirring of breeze.
I imagine dogs
and people, their utensils

ranged around fire;
the land burdened
with lumber of settlement;
blood-heat of habitation.

COWS

From compartment windows
they were fake, too far away
to be real. Friesians, shorthorns,
angus: painted cows

in a book of fields –
while on the train I rampaged,
shuttling impatience
through pages and pages

of green. Unexpectedly,
we'd arrive and land in a world
where they moped.
The first day up, a drover,

I'd goad them on with a stick
then savour their warmth
at milking when packed
into pungent stalls,

where a white jet steamed
frothed up in a galvanized pail.
The fields outside
were full of their muck

in pats that were ringed
and perfect. Wherever
I ran, that muck
would cling to my shoes.

HOLIDAYS

A treeless terrain,
it was neatly parcelled
by drystone walls
and ditches, mapped out

in identical townlands:
Carrickandy, Bohola –
names bright with
a garbled music;

and there I learned
I had senses –
the sombre reek
of turf stacked high

in a shed, or grass
laid down by a scythe.
Forbidden again
each summer,

I would climb up
to my grandfather's
hay, succumb
in its net of fragrance.

A HOUSE IN MAYO

So long abandoned, their house and garden
lay caged in the tangle of briars. As a child
I looked for secrets, creating new lives
each visit from what they had left behind –

a cartwheel found in a shed with scraps
of chains and leather: disused tackle
they'd handled. One gable down completely,
I pictured thatch that the wind had blown.

And rain had weathered that house till it showed
a harsh perfection the owners did not see.
Around it, their ordered plot ran wild
in a furious zone of growth and process.

Drawn to that absence, I explored it all
and forced a way through where tall weeds struggled
against me: the tough bright heads of ragwort
alive each summer in a haze of midges.

Empty houses were scars on the landscape.
Wild seeds blew in to heal them. When people
vanished, the tracks they had made were smothered.
Returning, all I ever found were mine.

EASTER 1966

On a brand new TV we watched soldiers
parade and saw, far off in Dublin,
the men file past in ranked array
while dignitaries took the salute.
In droning celebration, a band
thumped out *The Foggy Dew*.
Did their heads, too, drum to a bidding voice,
an identity: *Poblacht na hÉireann*
proclaimed in print on walls?

A die-hard republican veteran,
he had shouldered a gun in history.
Watching the screen with a child
half a century later,
he doled out his memories.
With good-natured verve,
he spoke of days he'd lived through.

Memorial pageant, a smokeless sky –
we heard crowds cheer in Dublin.
Spruced up in his duds, I see him
jauntily step into line.

A WALDORF SALAD
for Paul

The Waldorf was always Grandad's hotel –
the place he had helped to build but never
got to stay in. From his room in the Bronx,
did he hop on the El to leave his mark

on Manhattan's skyline? It's too late now
to check the details, as I try at least
to plot his absent years back from the splash
of its opening to the Wall Street Crash.

Working out his children's ages, a gap's
revealed, and then how old he must have been –
a Volunteer with mouths to feed, his goal
something better than the Irish Free State.

His cause in abeyance, he chanced his luck
abroad, where he found the future rooted
in its bottom line. He returned with cash
and tall stories, a few Yankee phrases.

But what did he make of bootleg whisky,
when he had no chance of a quiet pint;
or the well-dressed hoodlums and shoeshine boys
who had never crossed fields or dug a ditch?

Above his head the sky's a chart, criss-crossed
with girders, on one of which two workers
have started tucking in. A step away,
two waiters hover whose aim it is to please.

THE DRESSER

The shrine and archive of those who had gone,
the dresser loomed imposingly, hogging
its space – their one attempt at opulence
in a room that was otherwise spartan.

Ranged above it, in a gap left beneath
the ceiling, there were portraits of couples
who had tied the knot elsewhere: brides and grooms
in cheap suits they'd wear again on Sundays.

Pushed to the back of a shelf – half-hidden
behind unsorted papers and the pots
for pins and pens – a girl in a white dress,
her image silver-framed, clutched her missal

in a gloved hand, staring back awkwardly
through jumble. A repository for anything
too highfalutin for everyday use,
it housed the china they laid out for guests –

the loaded Yanks, who were distant cousins
trying to find their 'roots', or English kids
whose accents wavered between two places;
their mums and dads who were sons and daughters.

Stashed away, alongside the cutlery,
the lace, and a stiff, folded tablecloth,
there were biscuit tins that bulged with photos
in which the poses always seemed the same.

THE WREN BOY

I must have been having the time
of my life the year I started singing,
trying hard to remember the words,
but high on applause and silver.

In the lounge bar of a pub
in Swinford I tried out a repertoire
I'd culled from the Clancys and mixed
to a Home Counties hybrid.

Shock-headed, crowd-pleasing,
I might have been one of their own,
giving them back *The Irish Rover*,
The Woman from Wexford Town.

Lured by the promise of easy pickings,
I tagged along St Stephen's Day,
togged out as a mummer,
and welcomed for miles around.

Strapped across her shoulder,
my cousin lugged her squeezebox,
melodeon, whatever, down lanes
and over fields. At each house

we stopped I gave them my party piece,
while across the buttons and keys
perished fingers danced
like spiders on warm stones.

GOLIATH

The day I floored Mick Kavanagh
defending my granddad's interests,

we had crossed fields to reach the shambles
at the end of the big man's boreen –

a morning's adventure together,
if I helped fetch the sucking calf.

The deal sealed with spit and a snifter,
they were making the most of the visit,

when talk turned to boxing
and my half-hearted career.

I must have missed a wink
between them – when it seemed

the giant was set to renege –
just as he saw nothing coming …

However the calf skittered
across the squelching fields home,

my grip on its halter was iron,
my gum-booted stride transcendent.

THE MORRIS MINOR

A lustreless black,
it slept all night
in a shed with the relics

of a different era:
a crumbling harness,
broken tools, a horseshoe

nailed to the wall –
then gargled to life
on busy mornings

when we drove
into town or to Mass.
Down the lane

the old man nudged it
as it lurched on
wrecked suspension,

its bodywork
strafed by brambles,
until at last

he coaxed it out
onto the open road;
and all those trips

we made in convoy
across that rambling landscape:
Enniscrone, Pontoon and back.

So many kids
and so much lumber –
the whole bloody tackle!

THE GIFT

Speeches from the Dock. It's just a book
I have never found time to read …
One summer, years ago,
I picked it up to leave as a gift
for that affable, authentic, old man
who let us rule his roost.

With his tall tales and politics
his talk was a warm anthology
that told us where we came from,
that here it was we belonged –
the past enshrined for good
in its list of martyrs.
Wolf Tone, Emmet, Orr –
through his eyes I see them all.

Each shade impassioned
and free, they hold their accusers
spellbound, their eloquence flowing
in classical streams.

Our past was a landscape
perfected in memory,
where trees survive passing storms.

RESPECTS

Her hand at the door, my aunt
said quietly: *He's going*
then urged me in to speak.
Why? for I found him there
at peace, beyond all need
of words or comfort.

Without will, broken,
he was propped up against pillows
and, like a child, wore a bib
to feed. Sustaining nothing,
he slopped weak broth
from a bowl he could not handle.

Its warm breath flared.
It had no power that quickened in him.
I played a part ten minutes
– the quietness pounding its anvil –
and quit. My dying bones
were light as those of a bird.

THE LEAVING CERT

Mislaid for decades, I had never seen it
– the certificate they gave you the year
you finished school. Thirteen and biddable,
I doubt you had been much bother at all,
picking up quite easily the basics
prescribed for the life that lay before you.

Beyond the geography of small towns,
fields, and enigmatic hills, among which
your predecessors scratched out a living,
or moved away, you'd followed the Master's
travels, his pointer assertive on maps,
his 'memories' a well-intended ploy

when his horizons were limited too,
his learning shaky: a sprinkle of words
in a dying tongue, his high-sounding speech
and wisdom adding weight to his display –
though any time refinement failed, the strap
or a cuff would teach the clowns and dunces.

But there it is for all to see, the sum
of what you needed to know, entangled
in a script you never got the hang of.
A plodder in Irish, your English fine,
you've always been a reader: family
sagas, memoirs, whatever comes your way;

and learned enough doing sums to eke out
the pennies, those tougher days you had to.
Your sewing basic – good enough to patch
and mend – religion still sustains you,
making little fuss when those you'd nurtured
turned their backs and let it wither away.

Never admitting to brains, but smarter
by far than what's suggested on that brief
resumé, what was the spur to frame it
– quiet pride? nostalgia? – when it turned up
again in a box heaving with papers,
clutter, your children's own pleasing reports.

TRAVELLERS
for Martin

They were always there at the edge
of the town, an unhoused presence
we drove past on shopping-days
and Sundays in the beat-up Morris Minor
that our grandfather steered,
erratically, down the empty roads
across the terrain of our fosterage.

We knew from him we couldn't trust
a tinker, who would steal both eyes
from out of your head, and feared
the coarse importunate features
of the women scrounging in the street,
imagining curses they'd utter
as soon as our backs were turned.

Alongside a ditch lined by trees,
their camp was a smoky shambles
of wagons, pots, and stiff tarpaulins
stretched into makeshift tents.
Their stringy dogs and muddy-hued
small children roamed at will all day.
Their horses stood at ease.

Out late one night in our teens,
with no lift home, my brother and I
walked past them, making our way
along an unlit road. The night
country-dark, a black sky welded
to earth, our ears were suddenly filled
with the yelps of their dogs, untethered.

Panicked, we stood directionless
till one of the men came over
to leash them, his coaxing voice
like a neighbour's as he asked
which part we were from, our visiting
accent sounding alien to us
in the shock of re-established quiet.

JOHNSFORTH

I

There is no way back
to that landscape
or the child
that you once were.

The well is boarded up;
the Iron Age fort
bulldozed flat.

They have cleared
the table.
The fire is banked.

While you were busy
elsewhere,
they switched off
the light.

II

Níl aon bhealach siar
go'n tír sin
ná go'n óige
a chaith tú tráth.

Tá béal an tobair
dúnta; leagadh
an sean-ráth.

Glanta acu
atá an bord;
múchta an tine.

Agus tú cúramach
áit éigin eile,
chas siad
an solas as.

EPILOGUE
for Belinda

Clooningan and Johnsforth,
my terminal townlands –
when I think back
it's summer again:

the corn in stooks
like a redskin's village;
the swallows slicing
through miles of blue.

How easily then
we assumed our right
of entry where our books
and accent exclude us –

the snug interiors
where Christ's heart glowed
on a wall, delf ranged
on an ancient dresser.

Around the table,
foursquare, central, we sat
for soda bread, tea and cake.
Above our heads

from wedding photos
those who had left
smiled past, their features
fixed, yet distant.

MIGRANTS

Ships at a distance have every man's wish on board
Zora Neale Hurston

ANNUS MIRABILIS

It was the year that the Beatles invented
the good times, *the feel good factor* we felt
before the phrase was coined;
when the glossolalia of teenage girls,
mascara sluiced in tears of adulation, confirmed
for me that they were a different species,
though boys had rites of passage, too –
begging in vain to ditch my shorts for trousers.

The year had started with the Big Freeze
– as if the fires had guttered
deep down in the earth's core –
then drove inland a plague of sea birds,
the bottle-green shags I had seen in books
that hunkered by the gasworks
and along the Kennet Canal
like a bedraggled insurgent army.

There were goings-on in high places
and a sudden silence in ours
when I'd asked my mother for clarification
of what exactly a *prostitute* was
and, as the year drew to its close,
we were all together watching the news,
when a sniper's bullet
brought my mother to her knees.

THE FORBURY GARDENS, READING

Through a side gate whose unassuming frame
is draped in swags of pale wisteria
like hairstyles worn by Victorian girls,
I return to a half-forgotten space,
its neat enclosure more clearly defined
by flint walls than the past will ever be;

and where parched lawns, diminished and threadbare
in the unseasonable heat, mark out
a territory that can't now be repossessed –
the tiny fortress of Forbury Hill,
the bandstand's lookout, and the benched refuge
we reinvented as a secret cave.

Today even the Lion towering above
his plinth seems at a loss to justify
those fallen in Afghan wars, staring,
muscle-bound, into a sky where cranes loll,
ponderingly, raising disposable
futures from a debris of junked decades.

Like vague impulsive ghosts, those earlier selves
who rampaged in drab, unfashionable
clothes, our echoes trapped as a sibilance
in the tunnel that brought us, crash landing,
onto holy ground: a ruined abbey's
lost domain of ritual and trauma.

Hagiography and a dead language
bound us to our past, the tedium also
of a Corpus Christi parade winding
slowly through these gardens, the air heavy
with hymns and incense, my tired head mesmerised
by a thurible clattering against its chains.

SONGS HE SANG HER

I imagine their whisperings along grey streets,
trying now to understand what their courtship
might have been. Even the word is a period piece,
upright and earnest, like a pledge of clear intent
that starts at temperance dances
where he buys a cordial which she accepts.

He is skinnier than I remember,
though his hair is the same: the unruly waves
brushed back off his high forehead;
his Pioneer pin a piety that won't survive;
while she is so young. Then, as now,
all go and focused on living.

Marriage involves a letter from home,
parish boundaries, dealings with priests.
Holloway and Camden –
familiar haunts split by jurisdiction.

Then come years of thrift and children,
who will learn how their father
sang songs to their mother,
his favourite *I'll Walk Beside You*,
loved for its melody and because it was true.

CORONATION STREET

When days were out of kilter
between the daylight and the dark
our mother set a limit: eight o'clock
and bed, a watershed marked
twice weekly by funereal brass
that wafted from that blabbing
street, its title sequence vanishing
into a Land of Nod beyond
terraced roofs.
                    Trailing upstairs
to functional bedrooms,
we mumbled slipshod prayers
before plunging,
breathless, into chilly sheets ...

Late one night I am dreaming
voices: a woman still young,
who has her brood, and a man
who is buoyed by pub talk,
the *craic*, his cronies ...
Her litany's a wall
he won't get past until like us
he's learned patience has its limits.

BISCUITS

In this town where I grew up, traipsing bored
to mass on Sundays, The Kingdom of God
was also founded by men who believed
in teatime treats. Abstemious fathers
of a global brand for whom the darkness
was devils that winked and slobbered in drink.

The Good News a source from which to drink
the truth, it brought hope to the weak or bored;
and those worthies knew that sloth was darkness,
obscuring the plan envisioned by God
whereby the sons must face their fathers,
building a monument to their belief.

The Tale of the Talents, so they believed,
justified their faith in money, but drink
was vice, the ruination of fathers.
The honest grafter could never be bored
and to his family might seem a god,
keeping at bay the hard times and darkness.

The tied houses were spotless. No dark nests
of vermin, no leaks occur, when belief
is practical, for then the Word of God
translates to a staunch home with food and drink.
Progress with profits inspired their Board,
a decent world for mothers and fathers

to bring up kids with a field for fathers
to kick a ball. A warm glow in darkness,
and a little sweetness when you are bored –
these were the pleasures in which they believed,
sipping contentedly anodine drinks
of tea or coffee: potions blessed by God.

In a world where nations can pick strange gods
collectable tins could get goods farther
than these streets I know, to regions that drink
torrential rains or, when we're in darkness,
blaze beneath a single sun. With belief
so bright and firm, I too might not be bored.

A moderate drinker, relinquishing gods,
I praise good fathers for worthy beliefs.
What they abhorred was merely the darkness.

MONEY

What is it about money and the mystery
of where it comes from that takes me back again
to a clipped patrician voice and the lesson
my parents had scarcely needed to learn
when, reinventing the meaning
of home, they knew already
they had never had it so good?

For nigglesome years I bridled
at having to learn the value of money –
its grudging laws that set you free;
yet still admit to admiration
for the gangling tea boy my dad had been
when he pocketed hopeless bets,
working on the railways.

Our dad could always tell you a tale
about a fool and his money
with the unassailable knowingness
he'd earned as a self-made man
and didn't need a politician
to tell him more half-truths
about *his* pound in his pocket.

THE HOUSE ON ORCHARD STREET

A three-up two-down end terrace, its door
opening onto the street, Dad had paid for it
cash down, then filled it up with wrecks –
a seemingly hand-picked gang of failures,
who let the bookies collect his rent.
My mother mopped its cracked linoleum,
unable to sweeten air that reeked
of dodgy fry-ups and dubious sheets.

When the Department for Highways claimed it
its lease had long expired. With somewhere to go
a flyover soars above its levelled site.

ST JAMES PRIMARY, READING

I'm working back to the dreamtime
of St James Primary in sixty-three,
the occluded and innocent days
before the gadgets and money took over –

like trying to retrieve the original colours
of bright, ridged slabs of plasticine
from muddied clumps we used
for project work in the afternoons –

my finest effort the model I made
with Terence O'Neill of the martyrdom
of Hugh Cook Faringdon
that earned us two gold stars.

In our tiny enclave we were swamped
by history: a Victorian church,
where we crocodiled to Mass
on Wednesdays, praying hard for Russians;

and the airy, abandoned ruins
of an abbey that kept the secret
of a good king's bones, its wrecked
high windows hoarding space.

Boys and girls, we never discovered
the mysteries of the others' playground,
but chanted tables daily –
our paean to the god of rote learning.

GRAMMAR SCHOOL

It had all started so well with a brand new
leather briefcase, its status enhanced
by its clasp and key, and its concertina sections
for work we now called *subjects*.

The first time I opened it up
I got the whiff of weighty matters –
a prize that was only eclipsed
by the drop-handled racer

they bought to get me there;
and which was to prove almost fatal
when a juggernaut caught me
on its blind side, pulling off at the lights.

Two months later my bones
were fixed. The bike barely survived –
a few parts salvaged, then grafted on
to a botched-up frame

that was hand-painted, hulking.
Up Berkeley Avenue's slow incline
it sapped my strength
like a lifetime's disappointment.

'MENS SANA IN CORPORE SANO'

By summer term, our first year,
we had mostly survived –
working class migrants' kids
and a few posh Brits,
some of whom were 'paying'.

Ungroomed graduates
of a 'two tier' system, we got by
on *nous*. No practice packs
fetched from Smiths.
No parents pulling strings.

Once past the rumours of dark
initiation – and barely noticed
by older boys – it was books,
books, all the way, hooked
on the rituals of a new Parker pen.

With so much to learn,
I was hungry for it, and mopped up
elements, declensions, dates …
It was hands-off knowledge,
orderly and abstract –

the better half of the old equation,
as I tramped blank circuits
around Prospect Park,
or held back, clueless,
on a muddy football pitch.

MOVEMENT TO MUSIC

The line was our parents loved it –
the annual gymnastics and PT
display. We had to be sharp;
we had to be spotless;
we couldn't let them down.

In cricket whites and plimsolls
– three hundred boys moving as one –
we were knocked into shape
by a military type
we had almost frustrated to tears.

Extending pliable limbs
to saccharine strains of Strauss,
there wasn't that much to it
beyond the synchronicity mastered
in six weeks of drill.

But we were only the troopers,
a backdrop, to hand-picked
optimates, the hearties,
put through their paces
on pommel horse and bars.

Impressive enough in their terms,
they landed sure-footedly,
then rose up on tiptoes –
arms raised, chests out,
accepting applause.

A NEW SHIRT

In the Shangri-La of San Francisco
they called it *The Summer of Love*,

tuning in and dropping out
to a soundtrack of spacey guitars.

Bookish, shy, and too young
for a droopy moustache and sideburns,

I was hothoused instead by Hayes
for the maths I was taking early,

but got a hint of something else
in Scott Mckenzie's anthem.

Against her better judgment,
my mother allowed me to pick a shirt.

– A bright yellow shocker
with a floppy, extravagant collar,

it didn't survive the first lesson
before they sent me home

to dream on at the back of the bus
of topless Haight-Ashbury girls,

whose painted bodies sway
to airborne waves of music.

SUMMER OF '69
velut in pratis ubi apes aestate serena
floribus insidunt variis
Virgil, Aeneid VI ll.707-708

In the lightheaded lull between exams
we lay at ease among the roses.
Our striped ties slackened off,
our top buttons released,
we watched bees returning
– like souls from the underworld –
to Brother Simon's flaking hives.

The previous year in Paris
students had manned
the barricades; while hair tucked
behind our ears, or curled
subversively over collars,
we waged our own secret war –
counting days like sly insurgents.

WHEN SMOKEY SINGS

To get past the door to the Top Rank
disco every Saturday afternoon
you needed a suit, so mine
was a lifeless grey, a cast-off,
with narrow lapels that even then
I knew had never been fashionable.

Once in you were lost to darkness,
until your eyes adjusted,
bumping around the outer tables,
where you searched for mates
who talked big and smoked,
nursing Pepsi Colas.

In class we had learned
from Brother Vergilius, confused
and sheepish as we were,
about the risks involved in kissing,
how one thing might lead
to another, but somehow never did.

In the end the music got you
– Muscle Shoals, the Motor City –
making moves in a circle
next to a circle of girls.
Above it all the mirror ball
became your ruling planet.

STEPPING OUT

Sumer is icumen in.
Anon. Reading Abbey

Clapton is God!
Anon. Various walls

My new look that summer
was vagrant chic,
a stylized take
on Wurzel Gummidge
that had me sweltering
in a trench coat
and a battered
trilby hat;
my washed-to-rags
T-shirts finished off
flamboyantly
with a red bandana
tied around my neck.

In the Age of Peel
and Woodstock
altered rites
prevailed as music
filled the cloisters
I had paced
on church parades –
white boys
wailing blues
where late
the sweet birds sang.

GASOMETERS

I never understood how they functioned or why,
but a single gasometer beside the canal
brings back childhood. Leaning against
the railings, I see beneath me
the same swans drag their murky reflections.

Yet thinking back, there may have been more,
where now the concrete apron holds out
forlornly against rough grass and buddleia –
a listless space that might be healed
by the uncertain touch of money.

With a head for heights and a vision
I could be drawn to clouds up ladders
or go sky-walking around its rim.
Grounded, I see a stark geometry, the grace
acquired when things outlive their use;

amazed, too, by the thought of how
contraptions so huge and intricate can
be dismantled and then just carted away.
Like harmoniums breathing stiffly
I imagined them wheezing up and down.

Each time I passed the levels were different,
even if, like time, I never saw them move.
It seems that years are slow seepage.
They are colourless, odourless, tasteless,
as in some definition I once learned at school.

OSCAR WILDE WALK, READING

A rain-darkened gallery
of colonnaded trees,
it's hemmed in
on one side by brickwork,
opening out on the other
to a refurbished
view of water,
along which
commissioned railings
spell out their faith
in Wilde's *beautiful world* –
a perfectability
embodied
here in civic pride.

Though summer
again seems touch and go,
a *flâneur* might pause
between the showers
to take his ease
in a love seat,
watching a narrow boat
that just makes it
beneath the bridge,
as if it were slipping
through the eye
of a needle
or the darker
passage to Hades.

PEGGY

My aunt Peg was a country girl
who couldn't wait to leave it.
She was flighty, flirty,
and married a gambler
with an easy-going smile.

The first place they took her on
was a Camden Town tea room
where they had a Margaret,
so made her a Peggy
instead, as if that day

were a new beginning
among the fancies,
scones, and slices –
the serviettes and doilies
she insisted upon

until the end of her days –
like the fags that kept her slim,
out of sight in a wardrobe
long after, officially,
she had 'packed them in'.

In the photo they placed
on the coffin she looks
like a forties starlet. Her head
at an angle, she's staring
into a softer light

MIGRANTS

Rosanna Ferrario's mum and dad speak
with a funny accent. Just as yours
sound different to you because
they've come from Ireland.
Home is more than the house you live in.
They have showbands there
and do a dance called the Hucklebuck.

A WET BREAK

Outside in the street, where skies have opened,
a dingy curtain flaps across the day,
as rain beats down with blank persistence
on shining roofs of cars, dissolves
my windowpanes, bringing back to mind
for no apparent purpose a wet break
at primary school: how in partitioned rooms
with raggedy copies of *Beano* or *Dandy*,
we were fractious *Bash Street Kids*
with time enough to spare; and if an hour
seemed stuck forever in a non-event
of walls and rain, years have since
spun free, cruising blurred distances,
adjusted to the focus of each idle glance.

SHADOW BOXING

i.m. John Cooke

WORK HORSES

The clanking compound of the brewery
– where Dad did casual shifts,
when building work was scarce –
is buried now beneath the floors
of a multi-storey car park
and chat that drifts across
from cappuccino pavements.

Born to a scant inheritance
of rushy Sligo acres, my dad was bred
like his brothers to follow the work,
sending remittances home
from London, Reading and Philadelphia –
for worklessness
would have been defining shame.

And somewhere in the hinterland
of just remembered childhood
I am watching a drayman
as he guides heraldic horses
through a time-thinned stream of traffic.
Their sinews barely tensed,
they go unfussed about their business.

ASCENDANTS
i.m. John and James Cooke

They are on parade in perfect step
– my father and my father's brother –
strolling down a street in Dublin
where a breeze is freshening
and the nineteen fifties
are loitering round the corner;
and even if I've no way
of asking either how they spent
the day, or what claim
each felt he'd a right to make
on an open-handed future,
they are still sharp in Sunday suits
straight out of the movies.

Beyond that city, I can just make out
a cramped, pre-electric house,
where shadows swarm each evening,
and then the lane unwinding
through a bramble-obscured neutrality.
But these two, like shrewd apostles,
will leave for good a place
they'll later remember as *home*,
reiterating one simple text:
Self-help and Profit, a need for work
I'd like to think can't own me.

And now they inhabit an abstract
space to become such symbols
as I might choose to make them,
leaving much unanswered:
like who it was controlled
the shutter on that buoyant day.
A brother in Philadelphia?
– the disembodied voice
I heard on the phone years back,
who could have been my father,
or my London uncle, through
a hoaxing Yankee accent.

MY FATHER, THE PRAGMATIST

While scarcely political
in what you might term
the ideological sense
of the word, my father
acquiesced in the theory
that *the whole world
looks out for its own.*

Which meant that not
unnaturally, when he came
to vote across the water,
he gave his terse
but unequivocal assent
to the British
Conservative Party.

A united Ireland,
of course, would have been
his preference, but that
was sentiment and not an issue:
no shillings rang
in a patriot's
empty pockets.

And I remember how,
when I was ten or eleven,
our family relived
his war: he'd sailed
through the night
and just made it,
pulling spuds in '44.

Driving round Newark,
Spalding, Boston, splashing out
on B & B, we bumped
into one of his cronies
in some fusty, derelict
snug, where your kids
could drink inside.

Dossing in barns,
biking miles, I think
they had both been happy
when they found what seemed
like a home from home –
if only the fields
had been a bit smaller.

YOUR CHAIR

After half a lifetime of early starts,
and a few fly years that made you money,
you finally softened round the edges
and eased back, prosperous, into your chair.

It's there in our mother's place: a threadbare
seat of judgment, battered in the mayhem
of a clattery open house, its wrecked guts
sagging, its two arm rests coming adrift.

And fixed immovably in that still centre
you watched the racing on TV, shushed out
our conversations, as Michael O'Hehir's
gabble of names stampeded to its climax.

Another windfall? Or a better prize –
to know you were flush enough for losers
not to matter, in a different country
to have attained a gruff serenity.

That chair has hoarded the words you uttered,
and releasing them at times, as we make
our late decisions, can fill up a room
with some cagey, warm, and toil-inflected phrase.

Your chair is true north on a map of memory,
and points out paths, the sanctioned ways still worth
your approbation, the cuteness implied
in *Whatever would your father have thought?*

WORK

Any place we drove to, it seemed that Dad
could always show us the roundabouts, roads,
or paving he had once had a hand in,
back in the days he had worked much harder.

When he'd made his money and packed work in
he lost his sense of what to do with time,
moped around, got grumpy, and sent me out
to the 'offie' to refill his flagon.

A 'man's man' my mother said, who needed
a joke to keep him going, and something
to get him up in the morning besides
a late stroll to place his bets at *Coral*.

Once I'd married he told me that the years
he'd grafted to feed us all were the best
ones he had known, but how before too long
I'd learn that no one's indispensable.

So after he'd botched a shed, dug the pond
and built a rockery, the time was ripe
for change. With a clapped-out van and a mate
he started again on small extensions.

Marking out the footings or laying slabs
was all a matter of lines and levels.
You stretched a cord to breaking point and then,
to keep it true, you flicked it free of snags.

WORKING HOLIDAYS

All those years of it, the same
vague journey every place we went,
driving to work each holiday
in a choky, smoke-filled den
at the back of my father's Transit.
Life was the business of earning
your keep; no peace for a drone
in a house where you paid your way.

And each time my school books
were laid aside and the pencil-work
had ceased, it was back to early
starts, the strange renewal
of an intimate routine
as he poured impossible mugs
of thick stewed tea, turned out
a slithery half-cooked fry.

We'd wait together at the front
of the house for his driver
to bring the van, its diesel
engine roaring assertively
down the street. Inside,
they were studying form
in the *Mirror* and *Sporting Life*,
exchanging gargled judgments.

The steel doors slammed forlornly.
We were on the road once more.
If I closed my eyes I imagined
we'd make it to the next frontier,
when all we did was land
on a creeping new estate
where, opening up those doors again,
my gaffer showed me the light.

THE NIGHT OUT
for Paul

Going upstairs, I think of him still
in the bathroom, crooning. It's *Danny Boy*
or some doomed melody dredged up
from a past we're unable to share.
Nearly all of the words are missing
as he tries half-heartedly to reinvent them;
while the tune is sprightly,
pepped up for a night on the tiles.

When I played my records he told me
that music always needed a lilt,
a syrupy air you could hum
like a song of John McCormack's.
I was into the blues, the sax,
significance: no way that Muddy
or Dylan could sing!

His judgments were mostly like that:
definitive, unbending, like his sense of style
marooned in the nineteen fifties,
when the rest of us came along –
his wild locks restrained,
sleeked down with a blob of Brylcreem.

GAMBLER
Il faut parier Blaise Pascal

Bound over for playing pitch and toss
or, more portentously, *having gambled
on Her Majesty's Highway,*
my father was always an expert
at weighing up the odds,
made light of his brush with the law.
His gambling a science and pastime,
he never lost much, but knew
in the end that the world is flawed.
At best you could only break even.

He had taken us all to Ascot races,
and once took me to the Dogs,
where speakers bounced
their fractured echoes,
the track suffused with lights
and where, having placed
my own small bet,
it all depended on the hare's
mechanical, panicked blur.

Unschooled, he'd never read Pascal,
but knew what he needed to know
about risk, so went to Mass on Sundays.
The odds on heaven were evens.

SHADOW BOXING

The closest my dad ever got to poetry
was when he savoured some word
like *pugilist,* or the tip-toe springiness
he sensed in *bob and weave,*
his unalloyed delight in the flytings
and eyeball to eyeball hype
that went with big fight weigh-ins.

And maybe I should have been
a contender, when I did my stint
in the ring, my dad convinced
I had style and the stamp of a winner.
In the end I just got bored.
You had to have a killer's instinct
to do much better than a draw.

In the gym the lights are low.
It's after hours. I'm on my own.
The boards are rank with sweat
and stale endeavour. Shadow boxing
like the best of them, I will show
him feints, a classic stance,
trying always to keep up my guard.

THE ADVICE

It was just the two of us,
our classic scene: myself,
the son, and my father
handing me down advice
like fruit from a gnarled
centennial tree, its roots
fixed in the stony soil
of work and abnegation.

If we'd been Victorians
I'd have answered him: *Sir!*
but he was Irish
and I was Nowhere, moving
on to my teaching post.

An unlikely Polonius,
his maxims surfaced
through the burr
of his brogue –
*Just live kind of right
and go to Mass ...*
until, after all
those sullen Sundays –
*It might be bollocks,
but at least you'll always
meet some people!*

NAVVIES

A blasphemous horde of poachers
and drinkers the big money had spawned,
they dug their way through rocks and sodden clay.
Camped out like tinkers, only their brass
was missed when they picked up sticks,
following the track to another day
of drudgery and dirty looks.

Country lads and migrants,
their mumbles hard to follow –
who thought of them at all
when the band played and folk
clutched tickets for which they had paid?

THRIFT

Through white noise money has made
I hear inherited wisdom. It is battened down
and canny, telling me now to make do and trim,
as if somehow I might succumb
to the unforgiving cycle of extravagance
and meltdown. Stern-voiced, insistent,
it is penny-pinching, penny-wise –
peeking always around the corner.

HOSPITAL

Over and over his wife rehearses details,
awake all night, observing
the changing shifts, their faces.

Where air was pure
he lay at risk,
hooked up to clean apparatus –

its routine hum still audible
after his breath was spent.

MEMORIAL

In a windowless room they had laid you out
in a soft white bed of satin.
Packed in a huddle around you,

we had entered to see you displayed.
Your body at rest like a saint's,
no awkward warmth or gruffness remained

to stir its cloistered calm.
At one temple your hair had been shaved,
revealing a scar. They had trimmed

the growth that darkened your lip
to an unaccustomed moustache.
A gathered clan we stood, each lost

in a separate silence
until the drone of a rosary began.
Like a long abandoned language

its monotone rose, familiar, to beat against
bare walls: a cycle of mysteries
that couldn't explain or change a thing.

TO MY FATHER
ave atque vale Catullus

And so I send these words out,
faltering, along an unlit path –
as if words now

could urge a ghost
to break its final silence,
terse enough whilst living.

Or what do I know
of the life you led
the years before I was born

when, with a minimal
nostalgia, you quit
your Sligo outback

and earned your keep
in a country at war?
A potato-picking nomad,

a grafter, you biked
flat miles across
the Eastern Counties.

Your son, and now
like you a father too,
I resemble you

more and more –
born one country
and a world apart.

FAMILY HISTORY

I
Piety, reverence –
what shall we call it,
the quiet we make
in the noise of living?
We place cut flowers
in a hollow stone:
what emblems,
what resonant words atone?

II
In the end our visits
become a ritual
as Christmas finds us
clocking up the miles
to where his wife
seems as busy as ever.

III
And our children now
are a kind of gift
we bring along to share:
two growing sons
who scarcely knew him,
two daughters he will never see.

UPROOTED
Máirtín Ó Direáin

Our fathers and theirs
who came before them
found themselves at odds with life
in the struggle
to coax their naked rock –

content at least
if dour skies relented
and a shallow field
brought forth
its meagre crop.

To build a dike
or a dry stone wall
was each man's pride –
like a poet making verses
to keep his language alive.

And we now
who are their children
lodge in city rooms
where the landlord charges
to fix his leaking pipe.

Yet even we
will be remembered –
for the paperwork
we've left behind in our loathsome
government office.

CAVERSHAM

The wrought-iron
gates of its cemetery
swing open
and shut like pages
from a long
abandoned book.
It's there the chosen lie
in the acre we leased
from God
alongside Italians
and Poles.

Time has made me
a stranger to kin
I accompanied there
and souls whose
final progress
filled mornings
drearier
than those
I'd skipped at school.

(1980s)

CAVERSHAM REVISITED

I thought time had made me a stranger
to kin I've accompanied here
and souls whose terminal progress
filled mornings free from school;
yet now with those remaining
and some who've since appeared
I feel again a shared unease –
returning this morning
for the first time in years
to where my mother's loitering
on the brink of her sister's grave;
and the battered CD player
laid on grass pours forth
its thin lament in spite of drizzle,
impenetrable cloud,
and the plates of food calling,
over which we'll swap email addresses
and catch up with news,
while an octogenarian aunt insists
I haven't changed one bit
from when I was five or six.

APOCRYPHAL

My mother is always going to funerals.
She tells me that now it's all she seems to do.

Mass cards, flowers, the order of service:
'Sometimes', she says, 'they're beautiful' –

like the old girl who filmed herself
and filled a church with smiles,

piping up in a frail contralto
'Wish me luck…'
                        then waving goodbye.

FAITH OF OUR FATHERS

*Is gan sinn tagaithe céim níos cóngaraí do Shliabh Shíón,
nó Cathair Dé Bhí, a Iarúsailim neamhaí.*

Nuala Ní Dhomhnaill

MISCHIEF

I was prelapsarian and just curious.
I couldn't tell you the price of anything,

my jackdaw eyes twitching
at a glint of silver between the floorboards.

And later on there were camps and dens,
private worlds, like one I built

with a clean sheet and a clothes horse
lugged across the grass

and filled up with treasure –
the lodger's flashy cuff links,

of which one, suddenly pointless,
survived and sent my mother

on a hopeless quest. At the back
of the yard was a lock-up

raised on piles. It offered a space
that seemed appropriate

for my discovery of fire.
The flames were impish blues and yellows

that rose up triumphantly before me.
To this day my mother can laugh.

She calls me her Antichrist.
God knows how I ever survived.

FAITH OF OUR FATHERS

The creed we'd inherited, it was unambiguous
and always claimed us as its own
in a far-fetched calculus of chances.
Aspersion and charms
were tokens of our election.

And when our foreheads
were smudged with ash, it taught us
the word *mortality*, like a chapel
I've seen in my afterlife
built with cement and bones.

At the age of reason
peccadillos stamped with guilt
could be absolved in a box of whispers,
and purity of thought
reinforced in threadbare rituals,

spreading over our lives
a drab brocade.
Behind it all were generations
who had prayed like us and chanted,
professing faith in our creed.

Sustained by desperation and the certainty
that human ties will cease,
they had sought continuance,
their dreamscapes
shimmering through isolation.

THE MASTER BUILDERS

They made a prayer out of balanced stone,
the improbable height of a spire –
as if by risking Babel's curse
they'd glimpse the gates of a factual
heaven. The Truth was a presence,
palpable and massive, their skill
an arrogance made to serve it
with mathematical certainty.

In the shuffling parishes time
dragged, bogged down in the tick
of generations. Elsewhere,
violence spragged the ordered fractions
of a working day, and trailed
behind it corpses, smoking fields
of discord getting nowhere.

Vanitas: designs and frayed ambition
all that's new beneath the sun.
Pride, thus, raised each edifice
above its echoing pit;
and took the measure of stone
and dressed it, hoisting it up
until it soared like logic
into the high, unanswering air.

LIVES OF THE SAINTS

God alone knows why our mum had bought them,
a set of five thumping tomes with green boards
and gilt titles. The cross embossed on each
was emblematic of a better place –
while she seemed happy enough with this one.

In her small bookcase they were dusty slabs
laid flat on the bottom shelf. Never read
or even opened on a rainy day,
they were crowded out by flimsier stuff:
Time and the Hour, These Lovers Fled Away …

So when I was after a grown up book
this is where I started: *The Dark Secret
of Josephine, Cousin Kate, Venetia* …
Their covers mainly soppy – carriages
and bonnets – too much flirting spoiled the plots.

No lovers' games distracted Butler's saints,
who knelt down and prayed serenely on rank
and clotted sand, or otherwise bided
their time, single-mindedly focused
on healing afflictions, saying their prayers.

Fulgentius, 'shining one', Chrysostom,
'the golden-mouthed', were not the names of souls
who yielded. Accepting the final cut,
Eulalia's neck was like a fountain
from which, unabashed, a white dove fluttered.

PLAYTIME

One class at a time they let us out –
Miss Reilly and Mr McCormack
whose hand we had seen her holding,
and Mr Murphy whose wife she became.

In the days when grown-ups
were still in charge they always knew
what we needed: fresh air
and a space to let it off as steam.

Drawing blood on a regular basis,
the flint in the walls was lethal,
salvaged from an abbey
whose ruins loured above us.

To play the game of Chariots
you only needed a friend –
your arms locked behind you,
you'd skim the corners like Ben Hur.

The first shrill of the whistle
stopped us all in our tracks.
The second shuffled us into Years.

Any time we stepped out of line
was like a venial sin.
The mortal sins were dealt with later.

GOING TO MASS

I shuffled at the back
for years and kept a truce
at home by looking
at others around me:
the prim communion
faces worn like a mask
on dutiful daughters;
or the old women
who lit the candles –
crooning responses
from missals as though
caged from doubt.

Through pious
circumstance each rite
had refined us
in faith, but now
when the host is raised,
a tiny, weightless moon,
it drifts in orbit
beyond all touch of mine.

THE LATIN LESSON

With sturdy jowls Brother Athanasius,
who back then we knew as *Beef,* chomped great slabs
of Virgil, which he digested for us,
struggling with the English in Brodie's cribs.

Aeneas and Father Anchises moved
through a pagan world obscured by the toils
of syntax, while we shambled on, reproved
by a voice more urgent than the Sybil's.

The Brothers could all quote Latin, pronounced
with a palatal blandness, the soft sounds
of a church's dialect, and enhanced
their wisdom with words unscholarly minds

found locked in lexicon, drill, declension –
and those words are still the smell of incense
in a quiet house of genuflection,
tall candles lighting the untouched presence.

THE CATECHISM

Bored but efficient, I would learn
each week the allotted portion,
absorbing truths in easy stages
by courtesy of the CTS.
Who made you? God made me.

And why? as I paced to and fro
in my bedroom, intoning
like a mantra that singsong
of questions and answers
along with the rest of my work –

historical dates, irregular
verbs, the periodic table ...
Knowledge was the gift
of the Holy Ghost. A mediaeval
rigour gave shape to the mind,

a taxonomy of virtues
and vices, its drummed-in
certainties slotting together
like blocks: a flight of steps
showing the way

toward the Church Triumphant.
Goodness wasn't enough
when Socrates couldn't be saved.
Tridentine piety, a *credo*,
fenced in that perfect view.

I thought of Limbo babies,
and natives who had died
in darkness, though their lives
might be as pure as light
on unmapped sands.

PATER NOSTER

Our father which ...
How mere form
defined the distance

from *Our father who ...*
We would have gagged
on that one

recalcitrant pronoun,
such constancy
in our rituals.

Or should I admire
our passion
for exactness:

those dim,
theological centuries
when Church Fathers

dissected texts,
disputing clauses,
a single vowel?

The truly blessed
were unyielding –
they couldn't connive

to save their skins
and shocked
pragmatic pagans

who picked
their gods up
where they found them.

SCHOOLDAYS

In our purple blazer
and gaudy tie
we sat: the putative heirs

to martyrs' blood –
though unlikely heirs
tuning in

to the back end
of the Sixties:
the philosophical

drone of Dylan,
slick blues
from Eric Clapton.

The miraculous
our staple,
we pondered

the Shroud,
its weird reminder
of truths

that underwrote
our lives –
astride two worlds,

like Padre Pio,
we had the knack
of bilocation.

OUT OF BOUNDS
Presentation College, Reading

It's like I'm a truant trying to sneak
back in, fingers crossed and hoping
they'll never notice in the hullabaloo
unleashed by the bell
at the end of a morning's lessons.

If hawk-eyed Fidelis spots me,
or gruff Leander, should I own up
to my guilt and shock them,
knowing the slate is wiped clean,
if I make amends?

Too many decades have passed
since I first bunked off,
deciding nonetheless to risk it
past two minatory blocks
of concrete, their edges yellow-striped,

into a site 'protected'
by powers who've cordoned it off.
They have left a board with a fortress
logo and the number
to ring if I'm concerned.

Inside I follow blistered tarmac
that curves around a sunken garden.
There are no roses left, no hives –
only clumps of pampas grass
rooted in a dreamtime.

Staring blankly, the original house
seems stunned by its fall from grace –
the boarded windows, the silence,
its brickwork shot from the ground up,
revealing zigzag scars.

At the back the veranda's rusted,
where I see 'new' labs, the 'huts',
and older classrooms, past which
we walked to the 'clock',
awaiting retribution.

Toeing the line, we had no sense
that a canker, slow-burning
elsewhere, could bring down trees
at the edge of the field: their roots dissolving,
their poisoned leaves dispersed.

SHIPS

Drummed in by the Brothers
with medieval efficiency,
I had always known since schooldays
that *navis, navis,* feminine, *ship*
was how we got to *nave,*
its pews aligned in shipshape rows,
its congregation, facing east,
like pilgrims on a voyage
toward the promised land.

And on that Open Day
in the parishes of the Wolds,
when they unlock the abandoned
churches, I climbed the ladder
into a belfry that might
have been the inside
of an ancient sailing ship,
its timbers held together
without a visible nail,
its bell wedged and silent.

Like a fool or a sinner
who has set out on a westering
journey I looked across low hills
that heaved, collapsed,
and petered out, their green
swell disappearing
beneath unruffled sky.

LUTHER

I was taught to think of you damned,
damned in a pit with fallen angels –
Martin Luther: a name it was easy
to conflate with *Lucifer*. Yet now,
with a secular mind, I study your face
in Cranach's portrait to see what calm
he found in your turbulent features.
Irascible, yes, and blustering, but who
surpassed your self-contempt,
the knowledge that leads
to a choice that's existential?

And when the germ of conscience
ran to seed in a sprawl of discontent,
what could you do, but turn away
from rebels, their blooded boots
trampling fractious domains?
For you servility was freedom.
Translating the Word, you carpentered
psalms from rough-hewn language;
glossed epistles whose mandate
I have long denied, shrugging free
of your scarred century.

IN THE MIDDLE OF THE WAY

Reading again his verses in a language
I have yet to master, I deliberate
where syntax snarls, as page by tangled
page I check my crib for meaning.
There must be a path through it,
if I can work through detail,
and clearings lit by familiar usage,
their sound and sense fused and memorable.

So I start again from a dark wood
that bristles with analogies, though here
at least my text is clear: a solitude
where a dead poet parades his fear –
a locus read until it's got by heart.
He struggled against a falsehood,
while I stumble on words he wrote
to make his falsehood plain

who, like him, find myself
in the middle way. It's June again,
and the year charts a zodiac
that is for me a flimsy image.
A putative planet brought him comfort.
His science misconstrued it.
My northern sun presages only
yet another fizzled summer.

The middle of the way, and halfway
through the year: these are the tropes
I shuffle, seeking cadences of loss,
when for half my years a faith
like his sustained me, misremembered
scraps of knowledge that help me now
through footnotes, paraphernalia
of a poetry that's locked in time.

And if I've soused all that
in a sane Cartesian light, I know
what silt remains, what residue of fear,
aspiring only to makeshift virtues
of decency and toleration,
a relativism that in the end
might damn my dithering soul
to the swarm-swept Hell of trimmers.

(1988)

FATHERS

My imaginary shore glazed by visions,
fierce brink of intellect and punished sand –
Africa, where a jammed syntax loosens
to yield plain prose that the pure
might understand, the shrill province
a furnace where effete Latinity
is forged anew and each man's Word
thrives on diatribe, death-wish, sell-out,
the watery balm of reconciliations.

I think of Augustine wandering
the bleached streets of his indulgence,
his pleasures daily reduced to a scatter of bones
like a picked carcass the noon-haze whitens.
Imperatives sound his hunger
and urge him on to pick up, read, and seize
those sanctioned truths –
a momentary thunder filling his mind
with the din of certainties.

CALVIN'S GENEVA

Like a theological Sparta,
I try to imagine his city state
secured against all doubt;

and a mind as poised
and incisive as a chill
sentence from Seneca.

There is a blue lake
for contemplation,
and sky as clean as a plain text

above its huddled streets –
a fundamental crisp air
that nips your breath like tonic.

As each small press grows loud
in the rattle of inspiration
translations and tracts

gain ground, where tattered
fiefdoms coalesce
into the map of Europe.

Never graced
with ambiguity, conviction
wields its flensing light

and peels back
the stiff accretions
on hand-me-down morality.

ON THE FRONT

That bleak December sky, it's as cold
and unanswerable as the plodding logic
of doubt and schools our unkempt visions
in the levelling rigour of its light.

Taking my stroll this early evening
I walk past illuminations
that like the icons that haunted childhood
are dormant till night comes round again.

Today no cloudscape lures my eye
beyond this solid edge,
or hints at some lost home –
the domain of weird hierarchical choirs.

ON MY DAUGHTER'S CONVERSION TO ISLAM
for Anna

How strange when I, who inherited faith
and kept it like a shabby gift, outgrown,
and then abandoned, see how on your own
you have discovered a different path –

Islam, which, in the language you've studied
so well and love, I've learned has the meaning
surrender. You have seen light shining,
where I must shape my own less certain code.

Your daily prayers and recitation flow
serenely from the prophet's desert well,
a stream where each resonant syllable
is a pure sound whose music I'll allow,

noting again with pride the stubborn skill
you show in tracing its delicate script,
a calligraphy that seems implicit
in all you do, gracing the habitual.

And you held your nerve these turbulent days,
when you set yourself apart: your blazon
a scarf which, for some, affronts their reason,
now that zealots commandeer the airwaves.

It was not always so. Beneath the glare
of a Moorish sky I have looked to see
a formal garden, where geometry
and tempered light harmonize with water.

BEGINNINGS

So there we were in Camden, my mother,
my wife and I, on the day of our daughter's *nikah* –
when, suddenly, memories surfaced
and Mum was back on the stamping ground
she'd known just after the war,
a migrant girl discovering life,
blown in from the back of beyond.

Those days austerity seemed a lark,
when all the others from home
had made the journey too –
the men on buildings and roads,
while she and her favourite sister
skivvied in a plush hotel,
kept going by the weekend's dances,
where they both jitterbugged,
attracting their husbands.

I thought how with luck
a life may find its true beginning
as on that day we approached
the flat where another marriage
would soon take place.

The father welcomed us in.
I answered *wa aleikum salaam;*
and as our gathering moved
into separate rooms
I remembered the Mass at Swinford:
the men sitting on the right,
the women on the left.

PILGRIMS
for Ziyad, Tamim & Rafiq

When the day has come,
you will make a journey
to the city of Mecca.

Each of you a pilgrim
dressed in white,
you will cast the stones

that set you free
from Shaitán, the evil one.
Circling the Ka'aba

you will feel around you
the crowd surging
like a river in spate;

and though it's a distance
I cannot travel,
the scallop shells

on my school badge
made me a pilgrim too
like those who had tramped

to the far-flung shrine
of Santiago
de Compostela

AFTER HOURS

i.m. John Durr

AN OPEN DRAWER

I have opened a drawer in memory
revealing odds and ends, a treasure trove
of objects they may have thought
were useful, but mostly never were;
and laid among them the airmail letters
– light blue and flimsy.

Slicing them open with a kitchen knife
along striped edges, they eased out
the creases to read the news
from Sydney, Detroit, Toronto …
and learned how children prosper
that work is work and how,
wherever you travel,
you will find a face from home –

All the details of ordinary lives
translated by distances
to a gauche formality –
'Hoping, as ever, this finds you in health',
each aspiration couched in pieties –
'One day, God willing, we will see you again'.

And buried in that drawer
with bits of twine, ribbon, forgotten keys …
the mass card for a son who died
and never made it anywhere
beyond their glistening fields,
their moist low-lying hills.

LEARNING IRISH
for Patricia McCarthy

The first lesson was a womanly kindness
there to meet us at the gate in a storm
of fussed endearment. Calling us each
a ghrá, Granny welcomed us in,
her vocative phrase archaic
and guttural, its long vowel a rug
laid on a concrete floor.

Those days, the place, are a timelessness
resumed by two faint syllables
salvaged in a slow decline, the word for love
in a language I've tried before to learn
as when, mild-mannered, intent, my aunt
pronounced the numbers, years before she died
at little more than thirty.

I still have some books she gave me,
and a *Teach Yourself* I bought,
its dialect wrong, its phonology
strange to the ears of those I knew –
like my cousin studying
in a Gaeltacht slum, her letters
asking: *When can I come home?*

Ó DIREÁIN
for Brian Joyce

The day I told you I'd read him
you remembered you'd seen him once,
hunched over his pint, broodingly,
back home on Inishmore, when you

were maybe seventeen,
eighteen, or old enough at least
to get past the landlord's gaze
in that free and easy tavern

where, perched on the edge
of a swirl of talk, you listened in
to blether, blarney, *craic*,
never imagining then

your first words might fade –
though learning two trades,
you knew that one or the other
would take you away,

your eye as true as the grain
in wood or the faultless seams
you stitched for years
in Savile Row's finest suits.

And there he sat in the corner,
muttering quietly, as you observed him
watching a gull that settled
on some weathered post.

OCCITAN

Even language dies, its culture
reduced to signposts hoarding
stony fragments: Ribérac,
Carcassonne, Béziers and Montségur –

a scorched terrain once lit
by penitential fires,
where land-hunger and dispossession
were the mind of God imposing order –

enlightened vowels supplanted
by a graceless legalese;
and dabbling in that tongue
to tap a lyric source,

I heard the sound of a *planh*,
a keening note that rises
in Languedoc and Connemara.
I could see myself

once more, a bookish child,
deciphering a primal landscape
where Galway, Mayo, Sligo
were *Gaillimh, Maigh Eo, Sligeach.*

LOCAL MUSIC
Seán Ó Ríordáin

He heard a lilt in the speech of Dunquin
that wasn't just words and what they mean,

but a music that only strangers can hear
in the *blas* and cadence of Munster –

a fugitive air that's lost on its people,
and of which he also was unaware,

when he lived too close to its source,
tied up in its workaday sense.

It's a music you hear elsewhere in Munster –
even in places where a language died.

EMPTY NESTS
for Bernadette

After the years you've devoted
to care, absorbed in this and that,
you ask how it is we end up here
in a house cleared of secrets
and the phrases we don't use,

dropped completely off the radar
of the latest bands, cult films,
and the logic of their humour,
migratory birds who land off peak
in Vienna, Graz, or Moscow …

Today we're travelling south again
to polyglot streets in Holloway,
driving miles we've got by heart
until, midway, its mileage known,
we stop at accustomed services,

where we're met by Polish girls,
whose English has a lilt
they've brought from *Kraków*,
Warszawa, or a place in the sticks
they'd tell me if I asked.

Overnight they just appeared
in a second wave from Catholic
Europe, like the earlier droves
who embarked on comfortless boats
from their western island

and who, making good, made us
who we are, as we visit again
a city where my parents met
and where one day our daughter's
children may be poised for flight.

THE FLY PAST

A mid-afternoon in late November,
the air chill, the sky a vacancy
when, from the corner of my eye
I sense it, a flash of sunlight
beyond my neighbour's roof
that might just be the hint
of mischief that says
he's at it again, riding his hobby horse –
the Monarchy, the Lords, Democracy,
still desperate to know what I think,
when I'm too busy to care
and it's all been said before …

And then for days, the Red Arrows
that serve no purpose and cost us money,
so why wouldn't we scrap them?
– as out of nowhere
a squadron of geese flies past
like honking virtuosi, their V
in strict alignment,
and who in seconds are gone,
having made their presence felt.

LAST ORDERS

The first thing we had to clear was the one
he prized the most: the cluttered pinewood bar
he'd salvaged from a neighbour moving on
at the end of the nineteen seventies.

Embalmed in a gloopy coat of varnish
that set to a brittle sheen, it lacked retro chic,
scuffed down to the wood along its edges,
its surface crazed with memories.

In the days when family came to stay
it placed him centre stage, measuring out
precisely his perfect Irish coffees
or each medicinal dose of whiskey.

And yet, for all its high stool bonhomie,
we dumped it, an eyesore for the viewers –
then missed a convenient shelf, sorting mail
that even now in his posthumous life

makes him offers he can't refuse.
At the back were cluttered shelves that clanked
to the music of jumbled glasses
and the unopened bottles of 'quare stuff'

brought back from their hols by others –
when his own preference was Jameson's,
Paddy's, the rank *poitín* he cracked open
for us in a conspiratorial hush.

REDUNDANCY

The happiest days of his life were those
they paid him for doing nothing.
Selling up in the south, he moved north

to a cheap resort, where he had
all the time in the world
for setting the world to rights.

Walking and talking to strangers,
forever mooching about, he ambushed
all who listened, forced now

to state their opinions on bees
that buzzed in his bonnet –
his commissarial Soviet hat,

picked up for the *craic*
in a Sunday Market when the empire
fell – like the Brits' before it.

An unregenerate union man,
forged in the foundry at Ford's,
shaky hands compelled him to drudge,

unfit for trickier tasks –
but didn't stop him raking shares
in utilities Thatcher sold.

Along the beach his dog lopes on,
as he quizzes again, as if
for the first time, stooped figures

hunting for bait. 'They were digging
for *wairrms'*, he will tell us later,
but not before he explains to them

why his dog's called *Red* –
not for its pelt or his politics,
but short for the deal that freed him.

CHEMO

The six months they gave you and which,
in no time, became a year
are stretching out into another.

It seems that minutes and hours
are made of stubborn stuff. They are filled
with nonsense that keeps you going –

your repertoire of dud jokes
or the crazy hat you wore all winter
to show the world you hadn't gone.

The chemo chases through your system,
erupting here and there: your blistered throat
so raw, it quietens you for days;

the scurf that scalds
your face. You have shucked off
loosened toenails

and hold out your fingertips.
They are blank, abraded. You claim defiantly
that now the cops can't trace you.

ROUTINES

The simplest routines can save us, the phone call
a daughter makes each morning at nine o'clock
in which the words are nothing but tokens
worn to a sliver; or small change so valueless
you'd wonder why it's minted.
                                   But then,
like nothing else, the routine alerts us
when the call's unanswered and we try again
and then once more, knowing the silence
can be explained by a short walk
to the paper shop, or a problem with his stoma,
that stops him picking up, while just in case
we cross town through fixated traffic
to where he's beached on soiled sheets,
hapless and alone.
                        Through a night
of whispering, of resignation and last rites,
his daughter keeps her vigil
until he blinks and then returns,
from wherever, alive at his own wake,
flirting outrageously with his nurses,
and wondering slyly if by chance
he'd be OK for a *Guinness*.

THE HOME

Purpose-built for final days
and all that they entail
of good, bad, indifferent –
it lies at the end of a block drive,
power hosed and sealed against
the encroachment of weeds.

With its Mock Tudor fascia
of black painted beams,
criss-crossed and dependable,
it looms up to greet us
with unflappable cheeriness,
its brickwork proof

against the years' attrition.
It's there I see you still, resolute
and cranky, your good humour
seeping away, a clouded ichor,
as nonetheless, falteringly,
you raise yourself from a chair.

Gripping a frame that gives
you backbone, you take small
steps along the corridor,
unaware, as you concentrate,
of the bed-bound frailty of others
whose doors are always ajar.

Returning to your own,
you see through the window
horses in a paddock,
but then catch, excitedly, a glint
of foxes which we, too, make out
just before they vanish.

WHISKEY

Your eightieth birthday came and went –
the landmark it seemed important to reach
in the last days of independence
before you quit the house.

On a street where you'd lived
for twenty years, refusing stubbornly
to lock a door, your English neighbours
brought you whiskey –
Irish, of course, and spelled
with an 'e', except for the orphaned
bottle of scotch we knew
you'd view askance.

Week by week in the home you worked
through them, one ritual tot a day.
Down at last to a rogue bottle,
I decanted it carefully
into the empty of Jameson –
a triumph, I thought, of form over substance.

31 GARNETT STREET

It had always been a smart move
to relocate to Cleethorpes where,
down at heel and windswept,
its unassuming streets found time
to indulge a 'character'
whose lilting and incorrigible
gift of the gab was all
he needed to keep him happy.

Cute enough in his own way,
or perhaps just lucky, he sold up
in a bubble we never dreamt
would burst, and then
cashed in, a thrifty Midas,
on the north-south divide
with a crock of gold
he scarcely ever touched.

And now he's gone he leaves
behind him a house that's hard
to shift, a theoretical asset
that each month will seem
more trouble than it's worth
in long-distance fractious
pow-pows over a few last sticks,
or the lick of paint no one's up for.

EFFECTS

So this in the end is what it comes to,
the junk that remains when the best
is all picked over: his shamrock kitsch,
old souvenirs, his family name
inscribed on a framed parchment.

From the bay window we've cleared
'rustic' pottery we bought for ourselves
in our nesting phase, but then passed on,
unused, when they first moved in.

With anything else that's saleable
we'll box it for charity.
Whatever isn't will go in a bin –
like the binoculars I fancied keeping
but couldn't get to focus,
even when like a fool I noticed
I hadn't removed
the caps from the lenses.

FRENCH PARK

How many days of emptiness,
endured and then unnoticed,
before estrangement settles in
like unchanging weather?

On soft mornings your mother rises,
the stationmaster's English wife,
no longer even mindful
of how good looks and blarney

brought her to this pass –
with all her talents on the shelf
too fine to be of use
and two small children suddenly

more than she can handle.
She will write you letters
you will not see. The hired help
will ruin you. In time

our secrets bleed through
the myths in which we bind them.
Towards the end you'll learn
you never were abandoned

and how behind locked doors
querulous and lucid, she raged
at each request denied
by unsmiling, veiled bitches.

GOING HOME

Stage Irish, for sure, and patriotic
to a fault, you were self-styled *Irish John*,
defining yourself by allegiance
to a place that doesn't exist
beyond exiled memories.

Through intransigent years
of bomb blasts, reprisals,
you picked over endlessly
the bleak bones of history
with me goading you to tell me

why you never returned,
knowing contentiousness
was your delight, the devilment,
in a schoolboy who winked each time
they caned him. Fearless to the end,

you were ready to go,
and so I'll say goodbye,
trying now to get it right –
how one who leaves says *slán agat!*
and one who remains *slán leat!*

THE TIDE
i.m. M.D.

After the years of bitterness
that for so long went unassuaged

your imagined griefs,
your dissatisfaction, encroached

like a tide, as grey fields
of memory foundered

and the chart of your days
flat-lined to a faint horizon,

shutting off for good
the life that might have been,

reminding me now
that each day light forsakes us,

who will leave behind
a name, perhaps, and things –

a shelf of half-read books,
some brooches, rings,

a wardrobe packed
with outdated outfits –

the clothes you always needed,
but never seemed to wear.

VALEDICTION

As guardedly as ever, each
knowing the part we had to play,
we took our seats
in the crematorium's chapel
to plangent strains
of *The Minstrel Boy*.

And then the quiet,
as fitting words were spoken.

Towards the end your bones
had shed their weight –
the poor remains
we now consigned to flames,
the curtain stuttering
around its track.

Our floral tribute, a skilled
confection of white roses and lilies
lit by pink carnations,
was laid out on slabs
beneath a spatter of rain.

The fragile roses
would be the first to go.

CONNACHT

So here I am again, homing in
on a landscape that's abstract
and generous, a photographic
collage whose cut edges merge
into the myth of perfect
childhood, a gloss of kinship;

till all our visits to country
cousins, whose lyric speech
made changelings of our tongues,
are now subsumed into one
floating summer, still
luminous above those hills.

An English nowhere could make
no claim on loyalty, when we left
behind each year its grid
of neat, pragmatic streets,
its ordinary day a dullness
that had shrugged off history.

How we hammed an identity
and hugged it close like homespun
before each death and marriage
unstitched its flimsy threads –
knowing now that Eden
is only a fierce nostalgia.

AFTERWORD

HOW A HEART BREAKS

i.m. Martin Cooke
(2nd August 1955 – 23rd December 2021)

'Behold the fowls of the air'
Matthew 6:26

This is the way it happens: a voice on the phone
explaining that one we took for granted
is no longer there, that junk food
and countless pints that wrecked
your balance and strained your heart
became in the end too much –
even at your shuffling pace.

Refusing to put a penny aside, so long
as you could buy a drink, your hapless ways
endeared you to all: the ducking and diving
by which you survived, the crazy
pickles you got through.

Simply living from day to day,
you always heard what we were saying
but carried on your own way,
sustained by football, films and rock –
your knowledge of trivia
dazzling, your grasp of the past
decisive. In a house
of scholars you were a savant
in a different way. No fixtures,
albums or dates escaped you.

We bought our first records together:
I Feel Free and *Paper Sun* –
though the only match I've ever attended
was one I took you to.
Before you died you supplied
the details: Reading v Southend Utd,
with your team winning 4-2.

So farewell, Martin, at rest now,
surely, amongst the gentlest souls,
who never strove
or sowed dissension,
or stored up wealth in barns.

Printed in Great Britain
by Amazon